'A' LEVEL REVISION FOR SHAKESPEARE'S *MUCH ADO ABOUT NOTHING*: study guide

by J. Broadfoot

All rights reserved

Copyright © J. Broadfoot, 2013

The right of J. Broadfoot to be identified as the author of this work has been asserted in accordance with Section 77 of the Copyright, Designs and Patents Act 1988

Brief Introduction

This book is aimed at 'A' Level and GCSE students of English Literature who are studying Shakespeare's *Much Ado About Nothing*. The focus is on what examiners are looking for and here you will find each act and scene covered in detail. I hope this will help you and be a valuable tool in your studies and revision.

Criteria for high marks

Make sure you use appropriate critical language (see glossary of literary terms at the back). You need your argument to be fluent, well-structured and coherent. Stay focused!

Analyse and explore the use of form, structure and the language. Explore how these aspects affect the meaning.

Make connections between texts and look at different interpretations. Explore their strengths and weaknesses. Don't forget to use supporting references to strengthen your argument.

Analyse and explore the context.

Best essay practice

Use PEE for your paragraphs: point/evidence/explain.

Other tips

Make your studies active!

Don't just sit there reading! Never forget to annotate, annotate and annotate!

Much Ado About Nothing

Introduction to Comedy

Let's simply define the word 'comedy' for now, in relation to a play it means a form of drama with a happy or satisfying outcome, in terms of:

- plot
- characters

The audience might laugh at the end or during the play, but ultimately the comic resolution is the most important aspect.

What does that mean?

The characters survive mostly unharmed. Also, moral issues can be aired/taught in a light-hearted or tense way.

Typical Comedy

List of typical features of a comedy:

- Romance blooms (it does not die)
- Festivities abound

- Characters get married (usually after difficulties/separation caused by mistaken identity/misunderstandings)
- Comic justice

Comic justice

What do we mean by comic justice?

- Conventional society protected from villainy perpetrated by a fool, mischief maker or a clown
- Characters get what they seem to deserve
- Restoration of order – good rewarded, bad punished

Subversive elements

However, William Shakespeare always add his own unique flavour to any genre, so in his comedies expect the following subversive elements:

- rude / bawdy language
- cross-dressing
- naughty fairies

That's not to say that Shakespeare's always original in every sense: his influences will be discussed later. Also note, that in comedies, the outcome will toe the social line, or buy into state-approved institutions, like marriage. Subversive elements do not end up controlling the status quo. If that happened, it could not be regarded as a comedy.

What else makes a comedy a comedy?

A lack of sympathy

- sympathy should be limited and the audience must not care too much about the main characters. Otherwise, they will not laugh at a character's misfortune.

Stock characters

- predictable stereotypes that the audience can laugh at in a superficial way. For instance, lovers are usually young and beautiful; they will be united by the end of the play. Usually, the most 'radical' thing that lovers will do is get married. That in itself provides a comic resolution to a play.

What else can we expect in a comedy? A sub genre, which is either:

- pastoral, or a rural setting, or is a natural world versus a court
- urban. For instance, Johnson wrote about London and Venice. His comedies were cynical and satirical, mocking and judging people's vices, like lust.

It is also necessary to know the term, **'tragi-comedy'**. This could be defined as:

- an uncomfortable mix of comedy and tragedy

- beginning with a grave problem, so we predict a tragic outcome, although comic elements are present from the outset

- have a comic resolution with loose ends tied

- giving the audience doubts at the end. That's why Much Ado is often referred to as a 'problem play'.

Nevertheless, *Much Ado* also conforms to the conventions of comedy, as will be discussed later. For now, let's breakdown the **ingredients of comedy:**

- slapstick
- puns
- sarcasm
- sexual innuendo
- wit
- practical jokes

Looking through the play, you ought to find plenty of examples of the above.

One area that students seem to struggle with, though, is plot. Some are not sure of the difference between the plot and the story. Let's break it down into bullet points.

Plot

- more than just story, which only tells you what happened, when and to whom
- the plot is about how the story is dramatised - that is, which events will be shown and how will they be sequenced?

Plot choices

- **comedy:** delay marriage, reconcile families and reunite lovers (e.g. *A Midsummer Night's Dream*)
- **tragedy:** hasty marriage, alienated parents and bloody revenge (e.g. *Romeo and Juliet*)

Now it's time to discuss the themes that appear in Much Ado.

Themes - Death

Characters do not die in Elizabethan & Jacobean comedy, but death can appear:

- in the back story
- with satirical overtones
- as a potential cause for loss & grieving
- as a source of dramatic tension & dramatic irony
- as a threat, casting an ominous but temporary shadow over the comedy

Themes - Justice

Personal and private justice by revenge became illegal during the Elizabethan era. Yet, there was still some sympathy for settling dispute in the old manner.

Themes - Honour

To Elizabethans and Jacobeans, honour meant family and personal honour. Protecting one's honour was vital to social status and male pride. Men's honour was built on bravery and strength, while women's was all about virtue and their obedience as, after all, they were the legal property of men. If anyone's honour was compromised then violence was likely to ensue.

Themes – Love, sex and lust

Tragi-comedies present love as rescued from the jaws of death and tragedy, but end similarly to romantic comedies. Another thing to note is that parental love is rarely nurturing.

Comedies present sex as ordinary and sociable after marriage; whereas in comedies, but it's a fleeting pleasure and can lead to the protagonist's downfall.

Themes - Gender roles

The highest status characters seem to be young, virile men. This is evidenced at the beginning of the play, when the messenger is asked how many have died in the war, he replies: 'But few of any sort, and none of name' (1.1.7). In linguistic terms, he may be trying to initiate a formal register by speaking in verse; however, Leonato refuses to match it. Why?

Perhaps Leonato realises he's a medium-sized fish in a small pond: he doesn't want to get ideas above his station. Male does not necessarily mean equal high status especially juxtaposed against the 'honour' bestowed on young Claudio (1.1.10). In contrast, Leonato is enfeebled by age, and has been relegated by the passing years in status terms.

Nevertheless, he enquires after Don Pedro, and the question about tears effectively feminises the highest status male in the play. Leonato asks: 'Did he [Don Pedro] break out into tears?' and the messenger replies: 'In great measure' (1.1.23-24). The word 'measure' adds a sense of manly restraint to the act of crying, which would be considered feminine.

Then, Beatrice enters the discussion by asking if 'Signor Mountanto' has 'returned from the wars or no?' (1.1.28-29). Beatrice is mocking Benedick here, and perhaps macho posturing also, by using the fencing term for an upward thrust. 'Mountanto' sounds more like fashionable fencing than doughty soldiership, so she's effectively put him down.

She continues to mock macho men, represented here by Benedick, by adding that he 'set up bills here in Messina and challenged Cupid at the flight' (1.1.36-37). Now she's suggesting that Benedick has challenged the blindfolded god of love to an archery contest. Once again, the macho Benedick is made to sound ridiculous.

So how does she get away with it? Perhaps, it's down to her role as 'a Shakespearean fool', which doesn't involve being foolish. Beatrice alludes to that role herself, saying: 'my uncle's fool, reading the challenge, subscribed for Cupid and challenged him at the bird-bolt' (1.1.37-39). Beatrice may be referring to herself here! She has a fool's lack of respect and can offer a social commentary on the action. The fool in *King Lear* plays a similar role.

In this role, Beatrice feels free to continue criticising the macho posturing of Benedick, calling him 'no less than a stuffed man' (1.1.55). By saying this, Beatrice has twisted the messenger's words as 'stuffed' could mean a rich, fat, pregnant or even penetrated person. Now she's feminised her great rival and is winning the 'merry war' (1.1.58).

She even criticises Benedick's soldierly loyalty, by asserting that: 'He hath every month a new sworn brother. [. . .] He wears his faith but as the fashion of his hat: it ever changes with the next block' (1.1.67-72) By linking him with fashion, she negates his loyal soldierly qualities. Benedick sounds like a poseur extraordinaire and not someone to be trusted. There's a hint of the spurned woman in that outburst.

Women had to rigorously guard their reputation, so if Benedick had been successful with any advances on Beatrice prior to the play's action, she would have felt compelled to marry him. Had that not happened, she would rightly feel bitter.

Female infidelity continues to be a moot point throughout the play, and this is hinted at when Don Pedro talks of Hero to Leonato: 'I think this is your daughter' (1.1.98-99). To that, Leonato replies: 'Her mother hath many times told me so.' This is the first of numerous references to the dubious sexual fidelity of women. What does 'many times told' tell us about Leonato?

Leonato is on the receiving end of his wife's tongue: meaning he is being constantly 'nagged'. He's the archetypal hen-pecked husband, judging by these comments; however, we have to take his word for it, as we never see his wife on stage. She is conspicuous by her absence.

Meanwhile, it could also be argued that Beatrice's role as 'Lady Disdain' is quite conventional, see Spenser's Mirabella in *The Fairie Queene* (1596) (1.1.111). Beatrice adds to this impression by telling Benedick that she's as phlegmatic as he is: 'I thank God and my cold blood, I am of your humour' (1.1.123-124). Leonato defines her personality by what she isn't, saying: 'There's little of the melancholy element in her' (2.1.316-7).

These comments refer to the fact that, in Elizabethan times, medical experts thought **four humours** (or bodily fluids) determined a person's temperament. It was divided thus:

- too much blood would lead to person becoming sanguine, or pleasure-seeking and sociable.

- too much yellow bile would lead to a person becoming choleric, or ambitious with designs on becoming a leader. Yellow was also associated with jealousy and suspicion. This was the opposite to being phlegmatic.

- too much black bile in the system would lead to someone becoming sad and melancholic, or analytical and thoughtful.

- an excess of phlegm would lead a person to become phlegmatic or relaxed and quiet. In other words, Beatrice is quite snotty! If she has 'cold blood' she's phlegmatic, apathetic or indifferent to males. Given that she has a reputation to protect, perhaps that's a good thing. In some ways, it wasn't particularly atypical, as Gibson notes: 'Now as women are much more moyste than men [. . .] they will neuer run mad for loue' (Anthony Gibson, *A Woman's Worth*, 1599). Gibson appears to be saying that women are naturally more restrained when it comes to love.

As already mentioned, women could be considered to be infernal nags. Even today, the word 'nag' can refer to a horse as well as somebody that continually complains, trying to manipulate the other person. Even now, the word is largely associated with women. 'The nagging wife' is still a stereotype seen on TV and the big screen, see Hyacinth Bucket in *Keeping Up Appearances*.

Indeed, Benedick compares Beatrice's tongue to a horse with great stamina, when he says: 'I would my horse had the speed of your tongue, and so good a continuer' (1.1.135-136). Even more so than today, talking at great length was a stereotypically unappealing trait in women then, so Shakespeare is pandering to prejudices of his audience for the sake of humour.

Nevertheless, it often appears to be Beatrice who gets the last laugh. She continues with the horse imagery and makes a mockery of Benedick again by saying: 'Gender roles: 'You always end with a jade's trick' (1.1.138). A jade is a wayward horse that is able to unseat riders, but if Benedick is being 'ridden' then he's certainly being sexually feminised by the language.

Worse than that, Benedick still retains the very male fear of being cuckolded. This fear manifests itself when he mentions the blacksmith god, 'Vulcan', whose wife, Venus, had an affair with Mars (1.1.174). The institution of marriage is one to be feared, and he appears to be in no hurry to follow Claudio and 'thrust' his 'neck into a yoke' (1.1.189). Servile drudgery would follow for males ready to copy oxen, yoked together with another, forever ready to pull a plough along. All toil and no play seems the fate for a married man, according to Benedick.

However, Benedick still maintains that males dominate over women, when he says: 'I would not marry her [Beatrice] though she were endowed with all that Adam had left before he transgressed (2.1.229-231). How does this relate to gender roles in the Bible?

In the Old Testament, the very first man, Adam, had lived free from death, sin and labour until Eve's mistake. He had full control over everything, including his wife. Benedick is reminding the audience who is to blame for man's fall from grace.

Benedick believes females can be easily tempted. Not only that, they can undermine their husbands' authority with their constant nagging. Benedick believes Beatrice is capable of doing just that, as evidenced when he says: 'She would have made Hercules have turned spit, yea, and have cleft his club to make the fire too (2.1.231-3)'. Turning the spit was the most menial of tasks in the Elizabethan kitchen, so Hercules would be demeaned by carrying it out. He would be further demoralised by the loss of his club, which was was massive. Chopping it up would emasculate him. Benedick is suggesting that Beatrice would have even out-henpecked the legendary Omphale.

Beatrice seems to be ready to wear the trousers in any relationship she can be persuaded to embark upon with a man. In contemplation of that, she says: 'What should I do with him? Dress him in my apparel and make him my waiting-gentlewoman? (2.1.30). This echoes the fate of Hercules in the house of the aforementioned Omphale, who forced Hercules to wear women's clothes and spin wool with her maids.

Not many men would want to marry an Omphale. No wonder Leonato fears Beatrice will never get a husband, especially given her desire to dominate. He says: 'thou wilt never get thee a husband, if thou be so shrewd of thy tongue' (2.1.16-17). She may be cantankerous or 'curst', but she's not as full of black bile as the melancholic Kate from *The Taming Of The Shrew*, as Don Pedro notices Beatrice's 'merry heart'. At worst, Beatrice appears to be suffering from slightly too much yellow bile in her body, which is making her choleric and touchy. Elizabethans may have put that condition down to too much sun, so avoiding it would result in a pleasing change of nature.

Beatrice, herself, does not share her uncle's fears. She seems content to remain unmarried, especially as it will guarantee she doesn't become a cuckquean (i.e. a female victim of unfaithfulness). She quickly contemplates being sent 'no husband', and sees the advantages of not being in a position to be cuckolded (2.1.24). In that sense, she shares the fears of the males in the play.

As well as that, she's very fussy about whom she'll marry. She says: 'I could not endure a husband with a beard on his face!' (2.1.26-7). At the time, beards were considered to be a sign of virility and maturity, so her attitude contradicts contemporary opinions of what Renaissance women want. Shaven men were associated with deceitful, cruel eunuchs. Interestingly, Benedick shaves before Act 3 Scene 2. This suggests that he's lost some of his masculinity and therefore is easier for Beatrice to dominate.

Yet, Benedick is well aware of the danger posed by Beatrice, when he states: 'you shall find her the infernal Ate in good apparel' (2.1.234). Ate (pronounced 'Ah-Tay') was the goddess of discord, and would usually be depicted dressed in rags. Like Eve in the Bible, she was responsible for man's suffering, as she instigated the Trojan War by spreading discord, according to King Agamemnon. Interestingly, Benedick seems to find Beatrice even more alluring than Ate, as unlike the goddess, his lover-to-be is 'in good apparel' (that is, well dressed).

So fearful is Benedick of falling under Beatrice's spell, he volunteers to go on a dangerous long-haul trip for Don Pedro. He says: 'I will go on the slightest errand now to the Antipodes [. . .] rather than hold three words conference with this harpy (2.1.243-8). The term 'harpy' comes from Greek mythology, as it refers to a monster with the head and body of a beautiful woman with the wings and claws of an eagle. This suggests that she is duplicitous or two-faced. This comment also harks back to the earlier references to Beatrice being a 'rare parrot-teacher' (1.1.132).

The comment above also refers to Beatrice's loquaciousness but, in certain circumstances, men were also expected to be chatty. A male in love would be expected to be gushing with praise about the apple of his eye. Surprisingly, however, Claudio does not conform to this contemporary convention when he says: 'Silence is the perfectest herald of joy' (2.1.281). Here, Claudio's reluctance to speak would have been uncharacteristic of a typical Renaissance lover, whose passion would speak volumes normally.

There are other anomalies in the play, which cause one to question how stereotypical the characters are. For instance, Beatrice's sun tan seems to suggest that like her 'too brown' cousin, Hero, she's at odds with the Renaissance vision of beauty (1.1.64). As Beatrice puts it herself: 'Thus goes everyone to the world but I, and I am sunburnt' (2.1.292-3). She seems resigned to the idea of never marrying. She's exposed to the sun, literally and metaphorically, by not been house-bound. Instead, she's free to roam, get darker skin and become less desirable to a Renaissance man.

Themes – Disguise

Disguise can further or halt a love story. In Much Ado, Beatrice and Benedick's love is hidden behind a disguise of words, so it could be argued that it temporarily halts their romance.

I've been discussing tragi-comedy already, so let's look at the main differences between comedy and tragedy.

Comedy involves:

- stereotypical/stock characters
- a complex plot
- disguise & deception
- mistaken identity & coincidence
- pace (there are very few, if any, slow comedies!)
- a happy ending

We'll come to tragedy in more detail later but, for now, let's just break down how it essentially differs from comedy.

Tragedy needs:

- a hero
- a sequence of events leading to the hero's downfall/death
- a predominantly serious tone
- a sad ending

Some of the above tragic elements are expected to be found in comedy, as another thing that characterises it as a genre is harmony clouded by discord. One of Shakespeare's contemporaries, William Webbe wrote in 1586 that a comedy's course was completely opposite to the narrative path taken by tragedies. While tragedies would start happy and plunge into misery, Webbe suggests that comedies would start with a problem that would be solved. In his own inimitable words, Webbe wrote that comedies 'beginning doubtfully, drewe to some trouble or turmoyle, and by some lucky chaunce alwayes ended to the joy and appeasement of all parties' (Webbe, 39). That might not mean a lot to you and I, at first glance, but essentially it means that luck plays a part in making sure that mostly everyone is happy by the end of the play, if it's a comedy. Of course, he may not be thinking about then characters who caused 'some problem'. For them, a happy ending may not have been expected. However, for most it would be a case of 'All's Well That Ends Well', if we are to put it in true Shakespearean terms!

Another contemporary of Shakespeare, Philip Sidney, puts it a slightly different way: 'Comedie is an imitation of the common errors of our life, which [the poet] representeth in the most ridiculous and scornful sort that may be' (Sidney, *Defence*, 44). Sidney seems to be saying for a comedy to be effective it's important that the playwright mocks the characters for making mistakes. Those mistakes would be blown out of all proportion for the sake of humour.

The more ridiculous the mistakes, the more distance the audience should feel from the action on stage. That distance makes it easier for the audience to laugh, for as Sigmund Freud suggests, when we realise that the joke's not on us, we are able to release nervous tension by laughing.

That may be how comedy works on a private level, but it also works on a social level too. Back in classical Greece, comedy was associated with public holidays, so it's not surprising that we now expect order to be resumed by the end of plays that conform to that genre. For the ancient Greeks, comedies gave the audience a chance to release tension by laughing at action on stage that was close enough to real life to identify with, yet with humour far enough away from reality not to be hurtful.

Likewise, CL Barber sees the connection between Shakespeare's comedies and festivities. He writes: 'Much comedy is festive - all comedy if the word festive is pressed hard enough' (*Shakespeare's Festive Comedy*, 1963, p.3). Barber points out that during Shakespeare's time, people could enjoy themselves in a radically different way during May Day and Twelfth Night. No longer were people subjected to the same rules and regulations: they would be suspended for the duration of the festival. Back in ancient Rome, masters would serve slaves during festivities; however, by Shakespeare's time, Queen Elizabeth had banned excesses, like 'boy bishops' taking over church ceremonies for much of December. Outside the church, instead of boy bishops, a 'Lord of Misrule' would preside over drunken partying. This 'lord' would often be a peasant. The normal conventional world would be turned upside down for a while, for the sake of entertainment. It all harked back to Saturnalia, the 17th December in the Roman calendar. By the end of the Roman celebrations, just like a Shakespearean comedy, order would restored.

As well as the restoration of order, which is expected in comedies, as already hinted at, Shakespeare's comedies tend to begin with a problem in need of a solution. For instance, in *The Taming Of The Shrew* and *A Midsummer Night's Dream*, uncooperative fathers obstruct the path of true love. It is thought that both plays were written in the early part of the 1590s, whereas *Much Ado About Nothing* was written in 1598, a year before another successful comedy: *As You Like It*. One of the characteristics of Shakespearean comedies of the 1590s is their attention to psychological details, especially male suspicion of female unfaithfulness and of other men. In *A Midsummer Night's Dream* for example, Oberon's queen, Titania, virtually makes love to Bottom, despite him resembling an ass. By showing Oberon's wife being unfaithful on stage, Shakespeare is playing to male anxieties in the audience. As will be discussed later, this playing to male anxieties (or fears of being cuckolded) also goes on in *Much Ado About Nothing*.

Problem play?

In fact, this male anxiety is so great in *Much Ado About Nothing* that many critics refer to it as more of a 'problem play' than a comedy. It has been noted that the behaviour of the characters in the play is far from uplifting; instead, it could be described as the opposite. While the audience may laugh freely at the fairies in *A Midsummer Night's Dream*, who are inhuman and therefore distant from us, it may be more difficult to do so while watching *Much Ado About Nothing* which seems a bit closer to reality. The audience may feel a real sense of disappointment when they reflect on what has happened and what that action says about human nature itself. Although the play ends with marriages and the characters overcoming their distrust of each other, the lingering jokes about unfaithfulness leave a bitter taste in the audience's mouth. Rather than glee, there is a sense of unease at the end: hence the critics referring to it as a 'problem play'.

Comedic ending?

In fact, by the end of the play, emotions are still raw. For instance, Benedick and Claudio exchange words that could be interpreted as angry, depending on the production when Benedick says: 'some strange bull leaped your father's cow / and got a calf in the same noble feat / Much like to you, for you have just his bleat' (5.4.49-51). They had been at loggerheads, earlier in the play, and judging by these comments, they are not letting bygones be bygones. Benedick is suggesting that Claudio is the product of unfaithfulness.

He's going as far as suggesting that Claudio is the son of another 'bull', rather than being the son of his father. It may be amusing to the audience, but ultimately it's insulting to Claudio. It's lucky that the audience only feel a limited amount of sympathy for Claudio, who's little more than a stereotype, as otherwise Benedick's words would seem less comedic.

Nevertheless, this is not the only instance of an undercurrent of male anxieties continuing. Again the fear of female unfaithfulness rears its ugly head in the following comment from Benedick, near the very end of the play: 'Prince, thou art sad – get thee a wife, get thee a wife! There is no staff more reverend than one tipped with horn' (5.4.120-2). These lines are cut from some productions, as Benedick still seems intent on insulting Claudio. The phrase 'tipped with horn' refers to male sheep ('tup') and the sex act, as well as being a pun on the horns that were worn by husbands who had unfaithful wives during Shakespeare's time.

Form

According to Alan R. Velie, for Much Ado About Nothing: 'Shakespeare got the form [. . .] from the Roman New Comedy of Plautus and Terence.' By this, Velie is referring to the plot. The course of true love is diverted in Much Ado, so there is a parallel with the 'boy-wants-girl situation' found in 'most

Roman New Comedies'. Arguably, another parallel is found in the fact that the 'the boy is often a whimpering fool, and the girl is usually faceless' (*Shakespeare's Repentence Plays*, 1972, p.17). However, Velie is mainly comparing plot rather than characterisation: he notes that 'Shakespeare is far more romantic and sentimental than Plautus and Terence, but his comedies are similar in structure to theirs. The development of the plot - that is, the setting up and resolving of the central complication - is of paramount importance (18).'

Roman comedy

So it could be said that Shakespeare was influenced by Roman comedy playwrights, Plautus and Terence, who:

- continued Greek 'new' comedy traditions
- used eavesdropping and overhearing to push the plot forwards
- included stock characters, like Plautus's aging male lover and Terence's braggart soldier

As you will discover, eavesdropping is very important in *Much Ado* and stock character are found in abundance. In fact, it could be argued that Benedick is a composite of Plautus's aging male lover and Terence's braggart soldier.

Harmartia and Catharsis

As will be discussed later, harmartia and catharsis are important terms to understand for the study of tragedies, but the same applies to comedies. For now, let's simply say that harmartia is a fatal flaw. It refers to missing a target (that is, hamartanein), or getting something wrong by accident or mistake. As I've already mentioned, mistakes are fundamental to comedy. If you don't believe me, ask the great Greek playwright Aristotle, who says the errors that comic characters fall into creates comedy.

Morality plays

Aside from Roman comedy, it has been noted that Shakespeare was also influenced by morality plays. For instance, *Everyman* (a late 15th century allegorical play) involved the comic use of devilish characters and the idea of man being tempted by conflicting messengers. This concept originated in mystery plays. Meanwhile, morality plays depict temptation through supernatural mean, so differ from Much Ado in that respect.

Interpretation, setting and language

The critic Laurie Maguire notes that in Kenneth Branagh's film of 1993, the 'opening frames' frenzied domesticity – villa spring-cleaning and the airing of bedlinen – is juxtaposed with a photoquote from *The Magnificent Seven* returning soldiers gallop across the Tuscan countryside to encounter a household of women ready for romantic excitement (Studying Shakespeare, p186). Maguire adds that 'the play criticises and rejects romantic love as unrealistic, based on appearance and linguistic obfuscation (186). That final comment refers to the confusion caused by the language and double meanings. As well as that, the critic notes that Branagh's setting tells the audience instantly that it's a male dominated society we're watching. It harks back to the days when men were, if not cowboys then, at least warriors.

Maguire goes on: *'Much Ado* avoids the staples of Shakespearean romance: a green world, disguise, lyricism. Messina is neither a real world (Don John's rebellion is downplayed) nor a green world; disguise is employed for entertainment or mischief, not for self-protection and self-discovery; and the play is conducted principally in prose' (186). In other words, unlike *As You Like It*, there is no 'green world' in the forest. Yet Messina is not as real as it seems, for 'the evil' Don John does not really threaten society as much as we would expect him to given the circumstances.

Plan your 'A' Level essay

Say, for instance, you needed to write an essay using the following title: 'Shakespeare creates comedy by challenging the contemporary view of Renaissance women. Discuss this statement in relation to the Shakespeare's dramatic comedy, *Much Ado About Nothing*', how would you go about it?

Well, I always tell students to write the introduction last. The reason for that is you know the shape of your essay then and you can say what's coming up for discussion. For the actual planning, I would start with a definition (and I'd usually sequence it in the first paragraph following the introduction). In note form, it might look like this:

DEFINITION OF DRAMATIC COMEDY (INGREDIENTS)

- comic resolution i.e. loose ends tied
- moral lesson i.e. wrong-doers are taught a lesson, and everyone gets what they deserve
- usually marriages in Elizabethan and Jacobean comedies
- restoration of order

Useful tip

Link back to question at end of each paragraph and ask yourself: how does your point challenge the contemporary view of Renaissance women?

Introduction - exemplar

Much Ado About Nothing has been described as 'a problem play' by some critics. That term seems to suggest that the play defies genre-categorisation, to some extent. Therefore, in order to address the question as to how much comedy Shakespeare creates in *Much Ado About Nothing*, it will be necessary to define the genre. After that the focus will be on (list what you're going to discuss).

Paragraph 1 - exemplar

First and foremost, contemporary audiences would have expected their comedies to have a comic resolution. In other words, all loose ends should be tied up by the end of play. If that were not the case, the audience would struggle to consider the play to be a comedy. Secondly, Elizabethan audiences would have expected to be taught a moral lesson through the fate of the characters. Good characters would be rewarded with marriage, while wrong-doers would be taught a lesson or punished. Finally, the restoration of order by the end of the play would be expected. After a period of turbulence, the status quo would be restored, so that superficially, at least, the comedy would appear not to defy convention.

Paragraph 2 - in Point, Evidence, Explain (PEE) note form

P: Hero (conventional, submissive possession)

E: Antonio says: 'I trust you will be ruled by your father' (II.i.42-43)

E: 'ruled' implies ownership & 'trust' suggests it was commonly expected

Refer back to the question: does it challenge the contemporary view of Renaissance women? Answer it paragraph by paragraph.

Paragraph 3

P: Juxtaposed against Beatrice (atypical free woman, outspoken, defiant)

E: 'Signor Mountanto' (I.i.25)

E: ridicules Benedick

Refer back to the question: does it challenge the contemporary view of Renaissance women? Answer it paragraph by paragraph.

Paragraph 4

P: Beatrice is wild and untamed

E: animal imagery i.e. 'a bird of my tongue' (I.1.119)

E: carefree, without a parent. Also a shrew. Wild hair (see Branagh's film)

Refer back to the question: does it challenge the contemporary view of Renaissance women? Answer it paragraph by paragraph.

Paragraph 5

P: Hero is submissive

E: Act 4, Sc 1 'faints'

E: Shakespearean stage directions are rare, melodramatic for modern audiences

Refer back to the question: does it challenge the contemporary view of Renaissance women? Answer it paragraph by paragraph.

Paragraph 6

P: Beatrice dominates

E: 'He shows me where bachelor's sit, and there live we as merry as the day is long' (II.i.40-42)

E. defies conventional norms, seeing spinsterhood as positive

Refer back to the question: does it challenge the contemporary view of Renaissance women? Answer it paragraph by paragraph.

Paragraph 7

P: Beatrice dominates (2)

E: 'Kill Claudio' (IV.1.283)

E: modern audience can identify with her & feminist critics approve of her

Refer back to the question: does it challenge the contemporary view of Renaissance women? Answer it paragraph by paragraph.

Paragraph 8

P: Shakespeare conforms to genre

E: unlikely marriages

E: quick resolution is reassuring, but unconvincing and therefore subversive

Refer back to the question: does it challenge the contemporary view of Renaissance women? Answer it paragraph by paragraph.

Paragraph 9

P: Beatrice = clown/outsider

E: 'bird of my tongue'

E: outspoken critic of society's norms

Refer back to the question: does it challenge the contemporary view of Renaissance women? Answer it paragraph by paragraph.

Conclusion

P: Shakespeare challenges stereotypes through Beatrice

P: Shakespeare conforms to expectations through Hero

P: Both characters are used for comedy, as is resolution

Refer back to the question: does it challenge the contemporary view of Renaissance women? Finally decide. Don't be scared to sit on the fence, to some extent, as it's not a simple yes or no answer!

CONTEXT

Make sure you add contextual analysis to your answer. Here are some areas you might want to explore.

Subject matter

The tale of the unjustly slandered woman was popular in Renaissance literature, concerned with love, sensual power and marital intrigue.

Influences

Ariosto's *Orlando Furioso* involves the same kind of deception via a lady-in-waiting. Meanwhile, Bandello's *La Prima Parte de la Novelle* (1554) is a prose novella with a similar setting and names i.e. Messer Lionato of Messina, King Piero of Aragon etc.

Social status

Social status is one of the central concerns of the play. The lady-in-waiting, Margaret says: 'Why, shall I always keep below stairs?' She is effectively flirting with Benedick here(5.2.9-10). She's proud of her wit ('Doth not my wit become me rarely?', 3.4.63-4) in an environment where wit equates to social status.

Meanwhile, Borachio says: 'hear me call Margaret "Hero", hear Margaret term me "Claudio"' (2.2.39-40). From that, we could gather that perhaps they are both guilty of aspiring to be as good as their 'betters'! Note that at the apex (top) of the social pyramid are Don Pedro, followed by Claudio and Benedick. Don John is also a leader of men, with Conrade and Borachio following him.

The status of the women, Ursula and Margaret varies from production to production. They are 'gentlewomen' sometimes, but are maids in other productions.

Characterisation

The main characters in *Much Ado About Nothing* are opposites to each another. While Beatrice is witty and clever, her opposite Hero is passive and reserved. Opposite the cynical, misogynistic Benedick is the idealistic and naive Claudio.

Claudio

Claudio is referred to as 'Lord Lack-beard' (5.1.187), 'young Florentine' (1.1.10) and 'sir boy' (5.1.83). This gives the impression that he's:

- young
- anxious for approval of elders
- unsure of himself
- deserving of comic happiness?

Claudio is a lacklustre suitor, like

- Bertram of *All's Well That Ends Well*
- Proteus of *The Two Gentlemen of Verona*
- Posthumus of *Cymberline*
- Claudio of *Measure for Measure*
- Claudio's poetic phrases like 'thronging soft and delicate desires (I.1.227)' can be contrasted with Benedick's 'Would you buy her, that you enquire after her?' (I.1.133)

Hero

Like Claudio, she speaks mostly in verse. This makes their romance appear to be superficial. It is hardly grounded, like Beatrice and Benedick's earthy love, which is reflected in their choice of language: prose.

Leonato:

Leonato speaks 24% of the play's verse, which is an extraordinary amount of poetry for a 'minor' character. Some critics, consequently, see him as a protagonist of sorts, especially as Claudio speak only 16% in comparison.

Don John

Don John Is the product of unfaithfulness and, ironically, he is the father of the deceit that makes Claudio accuse Hero of being unfaithful.

Beatrice

Beatrice rebels against the male domination of Messina, which juxtaposed with Hero's more submissive behaviour makes her nature appear even more rebellious. Like Benedick, she shuns the idea of marriage, early on in the play, and refuses to conform to society's norms, like Queen Elizabeth I perhaps. She speaks **euphuistically**, at times, like Benedick. It's an affectedly elegant style of prose and not what you'd expect to hear from a woman.

Euphuism

The style comes from the works of John Lyly (1553-1606). In addition to the exchanges between Benedick and Beatrice in *Much Ado About Nothing*, both Polonius in *Hamlet* and Moth in *Love's Labour's Lost* employ a euphuistic style in their dialogue.

In a sense, Beatrice's use of euphuism shows she's competing with Benedick on his terms and winning the battle. This form of prose certainly suits a cynic. However, she is capable of moments of rhyming iambic pentameter too, such as when she declares her love for Benedick.

Like Benedick, she uses the following types of **imagery** in her speeches:

- classical mythology – harking back to a more heroic age
- animal, hunting, aggression
- age, death, decay
- clothing – which links to deception

Benedick

Benedick is a stereotypical misogynist chasing a shrew. Not surprisingly, he's a master of euphuistic debate. However, Benedick does switch to verse when he backs the Friar's plan (IV.1). Why here? Perhaps it is an honourable cause worthy of poetry. Yet, Benedick fails miserably when trying to compose a sonnet. Perhaps we should expect more verbal dexterity from a man who hails from Padua, which was known as 'the nursery of arts' where inhabitants learnt to argue both sides of a case. One of his favourite topics include debating a woman's worth.

A woman's worth:

- debated since the foundation of medieval universities
- gained momentum with the advent of print culture
- chastity was valued, but promiscuity was frowned upon, and women could go either way
- they could be thrifty, but could also succumb to weakness of reason
- while they could be heroic, women were considered to be the weaker sex and therefore relatively feeble

Nevertheless, once he puts his mind to it, Benedick wants an **ideal Renaissance girl**. This would entail her being:

- fair
- wise
- virtuous
- mild
- noble
- of good discourse (i.e. a good conversationalist)

After all, to the typical Renaissance man, the chief obstacle to happy marriage would be the **wife's failure to submit**:

- verbally
- sexually
- both

Loose words equate to loose women, yet not in the case of the articulate Beatrice! In other words, the ideal Renaissance woman doesn't give anything away, neither sexually nor verbally.

The predominant view at the time was very much influenced by the Old Testament idea of women as heirs of Eve, i.e. disobedient and therefore dangerous.

Not only that, the differences between the sexes was considered more pronounced then than it is today. Galenic physiology maintained that women were cold-blooded with a more sluggish metabolism and therefore prone to be more phegmatic.

How much Shakespeare bought into the above theories is a matter of debate, but his work seems to subvert contemporary conventional thought to some extent. In *Much Ado*, the typical bachelor (represented by Benedick) and the archetypal shrew (represented by Beatrice) hide their feelings beneath those very stereotypes. Both characters use those conventions as form of **disguise** or protective camouflage

In Benedick's case, his change from a cynical, misogynist male to a brave, chivalric defender of women simply sees him swap one norm of male behaviour for another. Therefore, by portraying this change, it could be argued that Shakespeare is mocking conventions.

In another Shakespearean play, *As You Like It*, male disguises liberate females. Yet Beatrice needs no disguise to be assertive. However, is there anything feminine about her? Is her eventual union with Benedick a surrender to the moral and social conventions of Messina? It's debatable.

The debate about a woman's worth is encapsulated in the title of the play itself. 'Ado' is a **euphemism** for the trouble suffered by a male character chasing women. 'Nothing', meanwhile, referred to female genitalia and also 'noting', which was pronounced the same in Shakespeare's time.

So what do you think Claudio means when he asks Benedick in the first if he has 'noted' Hero, the daughter of Leonato? In modern terms, he is eying up Hero. He fancies her. His desire seems to be completely driven by her looks, which in itself makes it a superficial love. As well as that, 'noting' could also refer to spying and love poems, which are littered throughout the text.

Useful information/Glossary

Allegory: extended metaphor, like the grim reaper representing death, e.g. Scrooge symbolizing capitalism.

Alliteration: same consonant sound repeating, e.g. 'She sells sea shells'.

Allusion: reference to another text/person/place/event.

Ascending tricolon: sentence with three parts, each increasing in power, e.g. 'ringing, drumming, shouting'.

Aside: character speaking so some characters cannot hear what is being said. Sometimes, an aside is directly to the audience. It's a dramatic technique which reveals the character's inner thoughts and feelings.

Assonance: same vowel sounds repeating, e.g. 'Oh no, won't Joe go?'

Bathos: abrupt change from sublime to ridiculous for humorous effect.

Blank verse: lines of unrhymed iambic pentameter.

Compressed time: when the narrative is fast-forwarding through the action.

Descending tricolon: sentence with three parts, each decreasing in power, e.g. 'shouting, talking, whispering'.

Denouement: tying up loose ends, the resolution.

Diction: choice of words or vocabulary.

Dilated time: opposite compressed time, here the narrative is in slow motion.

Direct address: second person narrative, predominantly using the personal pronoun 'you'.

Dramatic action verb: manifests itself in physical action, e.g. I punched him in the face.

Dramatic irony: audience knows something that the character is unaware of.

Ellipsis: leaving out part of the story and allowing the reader to fill in the narrative gap.

Epistolary: letter or correspondence-driven narrative.

Flashback/Analepsis: going back in time to the past, interrupting the chronological sequence.

Flashforward/Prolepsis: going forward in time to the future, interrupting the chronological sequence.

Foreshadowing/Adumbrating: suggestion of plot developments that will occur later in the narrative.

Gothic: another strand of Romanticism, typically with a wild setting, a sensitive heroine, an older man with a 'piercing gaze', discontinuous structure, doppelgangers, guilt and the 'unspeakable' (according to Eve Kosofsky Sedgwick).

Hamartia: character flaw, leading to that character's downfall.

Hyperbole: exaggeration for effect.

Iambic pentameter: a line of ten syllables beginning with a lighter stress alternating with a heavier stress in its perfect form, which sounds like a heartbeat. The stress falls on the even syllables, numbers: 2, 4, 6, 8 and 10, e.g. 'When now I think you can behold such sights'.

Intertextuality: links to other literary texts.

Irony: amusing or cruel reversal of expected outcome or words meaning the opposite to their literal meaning.

Metafiction/Romantic irony: self-conscious exposure of the devices used to create 'the truth' within a work of fiction.

Motif: recurring image use of language or idea that connects the narrative together and creates a theme or mood, e.g. 'green light' in *The Great Gatsby*.

Oxymoron: contradictory terms combined, e.g. deafening silence.

Pastiche: imitation of another's work.

Pathetic fallacy: a form of personification whereby inanimate objects show human attributes, e.g. 'the sea smiled benignly'. The originator of the term, John Ruskin in 1856, used 'the cruel, crawling foam', from Kingsley's *The Sands of Dee*, as an example to clarify what he meant by the 'morbid' nature of pathetic fallacy.

Personification: concrete or abstract object made human, often simply achieved by using a capital letter or a personal pronoun, e.g. 'Nature', or describing a ship as 'she'.

Pun/Double entendre: a word with a double meaning, usually employed in witty wordplay but not always.

Retrospective: account of events after they have occurred.

Romanticism: genre celebrating the power of imagination, spriritualism and nature.

Semantic/lexical field: related words about a single concept, e.g. king, queen and prince are all concerned with royalty.

Soliloquy: character thinks aloud, but is not heard by other characters (unlike in a monologue) giving the audience access to inner thoughts and feelings.

Style: choice of language, form and structure, and effects produced.

Synecdoche: one part of something referring to the whole, e.g. Carker's teeth represent him in *Dombey and Son*.

Syntax: the way words and sentences are placed together.

Tetracolon climax: sentence with four parts, culminating with the last part, e.g. 'I have nothing to offer but blood, toil, tears, and sweat ' (Winston Churchill).

ABOUT THE AUTHOR

J. Broadfoot is an English teacher and freelance soccer journalist, who also writes fiction and literary criticism. His former experiences as a DJ took him to far-flung places such as Tokyo, Kobe, Beijing, Hong Kong, Jakarta, Cairo, Dubai, Cannes, Oslo, Bergen and Bodo. He is now a PGCE and CELTA-qualified English teacher with QTS, a first-class honours degree in Literature and an MA in Victorian Studies. Shakespeare is close to his heart as he acted in 'Macbeth' and 'A Midsummer Night's Dream' at the Royal Northern College of Music in Manchester. More recently, he has been teaching 'Macbeth' to GCSE students in the Dartford area and 'Much Ado About Nothing' to 'A' Level students at a secondary school in Buckinghamshire.

Printed in Great Britain
by Amazon.co.uk, Ltd.,
Marston Gate.